THE HEALTHY VIRTUAL ASSISTANT

*HOW TO BECOME A VIRTUAL ASSISTANT FOR THE
HEALTH & WELLNESS INDUSTRY*

JOANNA MITCHELL

CONTENTS

ACKNOWLEDGMENTS

I'd like to thank two longstanding clients, Emma Sutherland and Amanda Daley, for trusting me as their Virtual Assistant and teaching me so much about small business and holistic health along the way. I'd also like to thank the hundreds of aspiring Health Coaches and freelancers who have contacted me for career advice over the years.

And finally, I'd like to thank my husband Kevin for his patience and unwavering support.

STARTING YOUR VIRTUAL ASSISTANT CAREER

NOW IS THE TIME TO ENTER THE FREELANCE WORLD

With the explosion of the internet and the ever-expanding virtual world, the category of 'work' is no longer limited to one job, one employer. Instead, the options are endless, especially for people who like the flexibility of working remotely, without reporting to a manager and sitting in an office for 8 to 10 hours straight.

It is now possible for anyone to successfully work online, location independent and create a thriving career. The recent COVID-19 pandemic has shown us this. The corporate world, which was once reluctant to allow staff to work from home, was forced into a remote working environment. In most cases, productivity was reported to rise, and many employees now admit to preferring a more flexible work life. Unfortunately, many jobs were also lost during the pandemic, unveiling the illusion that being an employee provides more security than working for yourself.

THE HEALTHY VA

As awful as the pandemic has been, it seems to have given many people the opportunity to consider entrepreneurship. Economist Julia Pollak says economic recessions can create ideal conditions for people to start a business. In the second half of 2020, the US and Australian economies saw increased registrations of new business names. With COVID restrictions and lockdown periods, many people had additional time and financial resources from redundancy payouts and government stimulus packages. The desire for a flexible work-life balance is here to stay and achievable in an online environment where start-up costs are minimal.

The Rise Of Freelancers And The Gig Economy

A freelancer is a broad category for someone who offers a service or works by the hour, day, week, or project. She is self-employed, and rather than working for a regular salary from one employer, freelancers typically work for a variety of clients or companies, either remotely or on-site, depending on the type of service they provide. Freelancers are the founders of the 'gig economy', part of the labour market characterised by the prevalence of short-term contracts over permanent jobs.

A Virtual Assistant is a category within the freelancing world. They are fast becoming an essential service for busy, small business owners who can't employ someone full time yet need an extra set of hands to run their business. The role is defined as someone who provides 'professional administrative assistance to clients remotely,' and services can vary from general administrative tasks to highly specialised services. Therefore, it suits those with corporate experience, keen organisational skills, tech-savvy, but not necessarily a professional background. Whether you want to become a Virtual Assistant full time or as a side hustle to your primary job, now is the time to dive into the gig economy and take charge of your career. This book will show you how.

Becoming a Virtual Assistant is the ultimate career booster. You will be taken out of your comfort zone, meet new people, learn new skills, and become more confident. I have been a Virtual Assistant full time, part time and casually throughout the years. I even freelanced my way through pregnancy and made the transition out of maternity leave slow and steady, just as I wished. It's been a role I have learnt so much from. Who knew I could create a website from scratch? That I could implement a marketing campaign and set up newsletters? I learnt all these skills on the job. I've also learnt how to run a small business – how to market my services, manage a small budget and ask to be paid what I'm worth. Sure, I could have developed some of these skills staying in my cushy human resources job. But, becoming a freelancer projected me forward, creating a work-life balance on my own terms, a future full of new possibilities, and the courage to try them.

In the following pages, I'll share essential knowledge on how you can create a thriving Virtual Assistant business and career too, and I weave in examples from my experience creating 'The Healthy VA', Australia's first Virtual Assistant service for the health and wellness industry.

SERVICES YOU CAN OFFER AS VIRTUAL ASSISTANT

The main reason people start businesses is for the freedom it supposedly affords. Yet, most business owners and entrepreneurs inevitably find themselves constrained by their business due to a lack of time to get everything done. Here's where a skilled Virtual Assistant can come to the rescue and step in to take various tasks off their clients' plates so they can focus on the core of their business. Take a look at some of the in-demand services you could provide as a Virtual Assistant today:

1. Inbox and Calendar management
2. Online Booking & Scheduling
3. Social media management
4. Online community management
5. Project management
6. Basic content creation

7. Re-purposing of blog content

8. Copy editing and proofreading

9. CRM database management

10. Client onboarding

11. Simple graphic design

12. Website maintenance

13. Webinar support

14. Email Newsletter support

15. Membership program support

16. Creation of lead pages

17. Email Autoresponder setup

18. Online program support

19. Podcast audio editing and management

20. Video editing and uploading

What to do when you don't know where to start?

If being a Virtual Assistant is a new concept for you, and you're unsure where to start, think about the 'Yes to everything' approach for your first client, so you can learn as you go and discover the type of VA you want to be. When I started The Healthy VA business, I approached my first few jobs with no limitations. By saying Yes to all client requests (within reason), I learnt very quickly:

- o   What I enjoyed doing
- o   What I didn't enjoy doing
- o   What my strengths are
- o   Where I needed to improve

- o And how I liked to work, e.g., hours, pace, and capacity.

If there was a task I hadn't done before (for example, setting up a newsletter), I was upfront with the client and explained that I was willing to learn. Many clients will show you how they'd like things done in their business, and some may even provide procedure notes. Approaching this new role in this way gave me clarity on the type of Virtual Assistant I wanted to be very early on, and from there, my packages, marketing, and terms & conditions started to take shape. As Richard Branson said:

"If someone offers you an amazing opportunity and you're not sure you can do it, say Yes - then learn how to do it later."

WHY CHOOSE A NICHE

A niche is a specialised section of the population relating to products, services, or interests. As a Virtual Assistant, I chose to work with the health & wellness niche rather than offer my services to any business in any industry.

Choosing a niche played a significant part in my VA success as I was able to 'hone in' on specific tools and skills required to meet the needs of the industry. I noticed similar patterns and challenges that health business owners experience and, therefore, offered a targeted solution (and eventually provided strategic advice and increased my hourly rate). I also attracted clients within the industry faster through targeted marketing, and word of mouth recommendations.

By choosing a niche, you become an 'expert' in your field and can provide specific, problem-solving solutions for your clients that are clear and concise. Achieving expert knowledge in one industry or service can also help you expand into other niches in the future.

"The best advice I can give to a freelancer is to focus on one area that they believe they can become the best in the world in. As opposed to going broad and spreading one's attention, they should go deep in one area. Ideally, they will become the person people turn to, whether it be for social media, WordPress development, or any other area. Once a person or company is recognised as being the best in a specific area, they then have more leeway to expand into new areas."

— Conrad Egusa, CEO of Publicize.

8 MUST-KNOWS BEFORE BECOMING A HEALTHY VIRTUAL ASSISTANT

1. You've Got To Have Your Shit Together

If you're the type of person who loves To-Do lists, colour-coded Post It Notes, and can maintain a certain level of self-discipline, then this game is for you. If you're scatty, forgetful and a frequent procrastinator, stay in the traditional workforce for your own sake!

2. Outsourcing Is A New Concept For Some Business Owners

In 2016, we saw the Virtual Assistant industry boom, as outsourcing became the norm. However, not all business owners are business savvy. If they've never used a Virtual Assistant before, you may need to show them the ropes and be their guide on how to create a positive and efficient working relationship.

3. You May Find Yourself Online 24/7

Managing your offline time will need to become a priority. It's a good thing you work for the health & wellness industry - a constant reminder to prioritise your wellbeing.

4. You Can Create Any Type Of Business You Want

There are no strict 'rules' on what you can and can't do as a Virtual Assistant. So, if you play to your strengths and solve a problem/need for your target audience, you can create your own job description.

5. You Don't Have To Be A Social Media Influencer To Attract Clients

There are many avenues Virtual Assistants can take to attract clients, and you don't need to be active on social media every day to do so. There are enough freelancing platforms to position yourself, showcase your experience, and attract clients. Word of mouth referrals can also go a long way.

6. You Will Start Drinking Green Smoothies Every Day!

If you want to specialise in supporting health businesses, you need to educate yourself on all things health and wellness. From my experience, taking a personal interest in leading a healthy lifestyle has been a considerable benefit when supporting business owners in this space. Before becoming a VA, I studied health coaching at the Institute for Integrative Nutrition. Many of my clients saw this certification as an added benefit as I understood their holistic health values.

7. It Will Be Challenging

Just because you know how to use Microsoft Office doesn't mean you can make it as a business owner. Freelancing is hard work. There'll be times where you'll consider going back to an 'easy and stable' 9 to 5 job. But all the ups and downs are so valuable in becoming a stronger person. With every high and low I experienced creating my Virtual Assistant business came the kind of personal growth I would have never experienced if I was still under the fluorescent lights of a city office.

8. You Will Love It!

It's not all 'sitting in cafes, drinking organic coffee in yoga pants'. But sometimes it is! The freedom that comes with being your own boss and creating your own income is liberating. We all have so much potential, and by freelancing, we can develop a career and lifestyle on our terms.

A DAY IN THE LIFE OF A HEALTHY VIRTUAL ASSISTANT

If you've spent most of your career working for a company in an office, you may be unsure what it's like to work for yourself, how to manage your day, and stay productive. So, here's a fun example of how I used to manage my workdays as a Virtual Assistant:

6:00AM-8:00AM

When I worked in a 9 to 5 corporate job, my mornings consisted of racing around the house trying to get showered and changed whilst eating breakfast on the go to ensure I didn't miss the bus. When self-employed, there's no need for an alarm clock as I naturally wake up with the sunrise and have ample time to do as I choose before logging online to start the working day. So, depending on my energy levels, I'll decide to either snooze, go for a walk or join a HIIT or yoga class. As a Virtual Assistant, you have the flexibility to flow with your natural cycle and moods of the day.

8:00AM-10:00AM

Time for a healthy breakfast with a cup of coffee, either at home or in my favourite local cafe. After breakfast, I log in to my inbox and task manager system to plan my day. If there's anything urgent to address, I focus on this straight away. Otherwise, I respond to emails before setting the time tracker to get started on my first task. When working from home, it's essential to be organised. Without planning your workday, you can become easily distracted, and before you know it, it's 4 PM. You've done two loads of washing, tidied your wardrobe, vacuumed the entire house, but absolutely no VA work!

10:30AM-1:00PM

At this time, I like to start meetings, either with potential clients hoping to learn more about working with a Virtual Assistant or current clients wanting to touch base on workload and deadlines. For potential clients, I always meet face to face over Skype or Zoom to work out if we're the right fit. A quick phone catch-up with current clients is sufficient (I'm paid by the hour, after all). Regardless, I'm make-up free, bra-less, and casual. Not a pencil skirt or high heel in sight! Working from home and meeting clients online means you can wear what you like to the 'office' and be comfortable. (But that doesn't mean you can stay in your pyjamas all day!)

Lunch

Lunch can be any time my hunger kicks in, and for me, it's usually the biggest meal of the day. Preparing and eating food at home means you can make healthy, conscious decisions, not to mention cost-effective. When you work in an office, unless you've prepped a packed lunch every day, you're a slave to the nearest cafe, which doesn't always offer a healthy choice.

1:00PM - 5:00PM

The afternoons are when I do the bulk of my work and when my creativity kicks in. It's surprising how quickly time flies when you're in the zone. However, I must remind myself to stretch or go for a 20-minute walk during this time, or my hips and back tighten up from sitting for too long.

5:00 PM-6:30 PM

Time to wrap up and prep for the next day. I reorganise my To-Do list and spend the last 30 minutes scrolling through various freelancer sites to look for more work. Virtual Assistants should constantly be on their toes and preparing for the months ahead to prevent their income from fluctuating. The ideal scenario is having several long-term clients with a good working relationship who can provide a regular income. However, if a project is coming to an end soon, you need to be prepared with upcoming contracts to avoid an income dip.

6:30 PM

My husband gets home from work. Having not spoken to anyone other than the cat in the last 5 hours, I get verbal diarrhea! Working on your own isn't for everyone. As an introvert, I crave alone time, and I'm more productive without the bustling noise and interruptions from an office environment. If you'd rather have company, search for co-working spaces in your local area. They're also an excellent way to meet other freelancers and potential clients.

9:00 PM

My husband catches me checking work email on my phone during what is supposed to be quality time. Oops! Switching off from work is challenging when you run your own business. There's no official start or finish to your working day. So, it's important to set healthy boundaries and hold yourself accountable for creating a work-life balance, even if you love being a Virtual Assistant.

THE FUNDAMENTALS FOR SETTING UP A VA BUSINESS

CLARIFYING YOUR IDEAL HOURLY RATE

As a Virtual Assistant, you determine the price you charge per hour or project. Unlike working as an employee, where your salary is determined by the company (based on the job description and experience required), you can determine what your value is worth to a client's business. It's important to remember that your rates are just numbers, and you can change them anytime. No one can tell you what to charge as it's a personal decision. However, it must feel right for you, as well as aligned to the market. I recommend looking at what other Virtual Assistants in your country and local area are charging to get an idea of today's market average. Many Virtual Assistants display their rates on their website, or you can simply join a local Virtual Assistant community group on Facebook and LinkedIn and ask what the going rate is.

Throughout my Virtual Assistant journey (which spanned 2013-2018), my hourly rate ranged from AU$35ph to $80ph and reflected the skills and experience I developed along the way. For example, I was charging $35 per hour for admin and basic organisational tasks at the beginning of my VA career. By the time I was charging $80 per hour, I was considered a 'Senior VA' and offered more advanced technical support, such as fixing websites glitches and managing marketing campaigns for clients autonomously.

Essential Things to Consider When Determining Your Rates

When setting your ideal rate, you must look at the bigger picture. No doubt you have bills to pay, a mortgage/rent, childcare costs, amongst other things. So, here are some things to consider when determining your hourly rate:

- What are your minimum monthly living costs - how much do you need to earn to pay bills?
- How many hours will you need to work to make the minimum monthly living cost?
- How many clients will you need to work that many hours?

If you have significant financial responsibilities, consider working elsewhere part-time or staying in your current job whilst finding your feet to ensure you're not entirely reliant on your freelancing wage. Feeling desperate for money when starting a new business is not an ideal recipe for success. I recommend always having a little nest egg saved for a rainy day. Generally, this would be the amount you need if you're out of work for a minimum of 2-3 months.

PACKAGING YOUR VA SERVICES

There are three ways to package your Virtual Assistant services. Each option will depend on your capacity, and therefore, I recommend offering all three levels of service when you start your VA business. Then, develop your preferred option as you become more confident as a VA. Remember, you can change and develop your services whichever way you want to; it's your business, after all!

1. Single Jobs

Single jobs are short-term work with a quick turnaround. These tend to be the lowest cost option, booked spontaneously. For example, when a client needs just a couple of hours support. You can also set a minimum number of hours for single jobs, for example, no less than 5 hours of work, to make it more financially worthwhile.

THE HEALTHY VA

2. Monthly Work

This package is a minimum number of hours per month. For example, a minimum of 10 hours, 15 hours, or 20 hours per month, paid via monthly invoices or direct debit. Any additional work outside of these hours can be charged separately. Working with clients on a regular, ongoing basis is the ideal solution for consistent income. In addition, monthly work enables you to build long-lasting relationships and foresee future income.

3. Project Work

Project work is different from single jobs as the working relationship tends to last a month or more, and you focus on a specific business goal, such as supporting a client to run an online program. Project work can be charged as a total sum of hours per project or hours per month of the project duration.

MASTERING THE ART OF TIME TRACKING

As a Virtual Assistant, you will mainly work on an hourly basis and charge a per-hour rate. Therefore, you must have efficient time tracking tools and systems to ensure you capture all the work completed. Here are my two favourite time trackers:

TOGGL

www.gettoggle.com/

Toggl is affordable and a great starting point. You can download the tool as a phone and desktop app and connect it to your browser. You can also track time against separate 'Workspace' settings, create Projects and integrate the data with task management tools like Asana.

HARVEST

www.getharvest.com/

Harvest is your next step up and my favourite out of the two. Like Toggl, it integrates with your browsers, phone and desktop app, as well as task management tools. However, its additional features include setting project 'budgets' so you can be notified automatically by email if you have reached 80% of a client's time budget. It also has an invoice feature that you can integrate with Paypal and record business expenses (more about Payment terms in later chapters.)

If you've not worked in a time tracking capacity before, it can take some getting used to, but once you've tried using a tracking system like the above, it'll become second nature and help to keep you focused on the task at hand.

Time Tracking Estimates

How long you take to complete specific tasks will vary depending on your experience. Use the list below as a guide on how long tasks may take and for quoting client work. Create your own list and adjust the time estimates as you become more experienced.

Task/Job Time Estimate

- o Uploading a blog post to a website, formatting, etc - 15-20 minutes
- o Creating 1 Newsletter - 30 minutes
- o Scheduling 7 Facebook posts - 45 minutes
- o Creating three social media images in Canva - 30-45 minutes
- o Minor website edits - 15 minutes+
- o Creating a 4 page PDF document - 1-2 hours
- o Setting up a 6-email automated sequence - 2 hours

- o Setting up a Webinar (not including hosting) - 15 minutes
- o Proofreading a 500-word blog post - 15 minutes+

Best Practice Tips for Time Tracking

1. Charge Your Time In The Moment

Have your time tracker on while you're working, rather than manually adding blocks of time to the system after the work is completed. So often, when added manually, we forget how long we've spent on a task and track time inaccurately.

2. Track One Client At A Time

Try not to jump between different clients while time tracking and instead focus on one client at a time. For example, spend 2 hours tracking work for Client A and then finish another 2 hours tracking work for Client B. You'll be much more productive this way.

3. Over Quote, Rather Than Under Quote Your Time

The intention is not to quote 20 hours when you know the job will only take 10 hours to complete. Instead, give yourself wiggle room for unexpected challenges and additional client requirements. It's better to overestimate the time it'll take you to do tasks rather than underestimate and end up doing work for free. If you manage to finish a job within the quoted time, offer some additional support and demonstrate how efficient and proactive you are.

4. Track Email Correspondence, When Applicable

Billable time is often lost when corresponding with clients by email or phone. For example, going back and forth to clarify project details can take anywhere from 10 minutes to 45 minutes in one day, depending on the conversation. If you feel you've spent significant time on the phone or email during the week, consider adding up to 30 minutes to your time tracker at the end of the week as 'general admin.' As Virtual Assistants, we don't have the luxury of being paid for just being in the office, like we are as an employee. Therefore, all time spent on client work is considered billable.

Staying Organised With Time Tracking

With most time trackers, you can set up different projects and job names for each client. Categorising jobs will help you reflect on your workload, for example, to see how much time you're spending on specific tasks. It will also help you keep track of the number of hours you're doing for each client, and if a client ever wants to review your workload or questions an invoice, you can export a detailed report of the time spent on their business. I recommend creating a maximum of 10 categories, each covering a broad scope of the work a Virtual Assistant can offer.

Here's a list of 9 categories to consider:

- o Blog - Tasks relating to blog posts, such as proofreading, uploading, formatting, etc.
- o Creative - Tasks related to creative work, such as social media graphics and branded presentations.
- o Meetings/Phone Calls - Client meetings by phone or Skype, etc.
- o Email Marketing - Any tasks related to newsletters and email automation.

o Other Admin - General correspondence, emails, and data inputting.

o Technical - CRM management, editing websites, and other technical work.

o Research - Research for blogs and market research.

o Social Media - Creating social media posts and scheduling.

o Webinars - Setting up and hosting webinars or video conferences.

MANAGING YOUR
FINANCES

It's essential to keep track of both your income and expenses. Not only will this make tax time much easier, but it will also help you develop a comfortable relationship with your finances and become aware of how well your business is doing.

For the first year as a Virtual Assistant, I used an Excel spreadsheet to track my business accounts before eventually moving on to an online accounting software. Visit www.thehealthyva.com/book-resources for a copy of this spreadsheet template, which includes example clients and expenses so you can see a demo in action. When tracking your accounts in a spreadsheet, make sure you keep the receipts for business-related expenses so you can reconcile the transaction at the end of the year. As your income and expenses increase, you may feel ready to set up an accounting software, so all invoices and payments are automatically recorded.

Business Expenses

Your total sales income is known as your Gross Profit, but when you subtract your expenses from this total, the amount is known as your Net Profit. Net is the take-home income you have made and is what determines the health of your business. For example, your Gross profit for the month may be $5,000 worth of sales, but if your expenses for that month are $4000, then the business has only made $1000 that month and, therefore, not as profitable as it seems. So, it's crucial to track your expenses to ensure you spend within your means and try to keep outgoings to a minimum. In the spreadsheet template above, I have included an expenses template on the second sheet tab.

Generally, as a virtual business, your expenses will be much less than a brick-and-mortar business. Here are some examples of the expenses to record, many of which are tax-deductible:

- o Advertising - Facebook/Instagram advertising.
- o Cost of Goods Sold - Online tools or software you may need to purchase to complete a specific job.
- o Education & Business Development - Books, business courses, networking events, business coaching sessions, etc.
- o Entertainment - Coffee or lunches with clients or business acquaintances, lunches taken whilst attending conferences/events, etc.
- o Office Stationery - Laptop, printer, notepads, pens, office chair, desk lamp, pinboard, etc.

THE HEALTHY VA

- o Subscriptions - All monthly or annual costs like website domains, time tracking software, email, and online storage subscriptions, etc.
- o Travel - Taxi or bus/train tickets to networking events, conferences, trips to meet clients, etc.

You can also include the following items as tax-deductible expenses. I tend to record them at the end of the year and base the cost on a percentage or proportion of the total annual expenditure:

- o Rent/Mortgage - a percentage of your home rent or mortgage based on the square metre of your 'office space'. You can also include costs of co-working spaces you may use.
- o Phone bill - a percentage of your mobile phone bill which you use to speak to clients.
- o Home internet - a percentage of your home internet bill.

Your accountant or tax consultant will be able to advise you further on tax-deductible expenses for your country and circumstances.

CLIENT CONTRACTS & PAYMENT TERMS

Providing clients with a contract enables you to lay out the scope of your work, as well as clarify your quote or estimated price, payment terms, and when the working relationship starts and ends. Ensure the client signs and returns the contract to you before commencing any work for them. Go to www.thehealthyva.com/book-resources to download a Client Contract Template.

Essential Payment Terms for Getting Paid on Time

You can implement simple terms into your business to ensure financial transactions with clients run as smoothly as possible. Firstly, I recommend always getting paid before you start any work for a client so you can,

- avoid having to chase payments after a job is complete
- avoid client micro-managing

○ can pay your bills on time

○ can lock in your workload for the next few weeks or months.

Can you ask to be paid first? Yes! It's your business. You set your payment terms.

If you are working with a client on a monthly basis, I recommend charging them for the agreed monthly hours in advance. Any additional hours worked can be charged in arrears. If a client doesn't want to pay the total for a Project or Single Job upfront, then you can offer to split the cost over two invoices or pay a deposit. However, just make sure you follow up on the remaining payment once the job is complete.

Deposits

If you have agreed to work with a client, but the start date isn't for a few weeks or months, request a deposit (e.g. 25% of the invoice) to reserve your time. By doing this, if a client pulls out at the last minute, it ensures you're compensated for any other work you've turned down to meet their needs. By paying a deposit, the client commits to working with you, and therefore, you have the right to refuse a refund should they withdraw from the contract before it commences.

Charging for additional hours

Sometimes, we quote for a job, but then we can foresee needing additional hours beyond the scope of the initial agreement once the project commences. In this instance, always notify the client before starting additional work and hours to clarify that you will be charging extra. Ensure you have their approval in writing so you can refer to the email if there's any confusion at a later stage.

Payment Terms & Conditions

Ensure you clearly state your payment terms on your invoice as well as in your contract, for example:

'Payment of this invoice is due within 14 days of the invoice date.'

It's also a good idea to clearly state your refund policy on your invoice and contracts too, for example:

'The Healthy VA reserves the right to refuse a refund for any hours completed before the end of the project or month.'

You can choose to provide a partial refund in certain circumstances which prevent the project from being completed. Go to www.thehealthyva.com/book-resources to download the Invoice Template.

Payment Gateways

There are various ways to get paid, and some are more suitable at different stages in your business. Direct Bank Transfer and Paypal payment methods are the most straightforward solutions. As your business grows, you may consider taking direct debits for long term monthly clients. Therefore, choosing payment gateways like Stripe or Eway is your best option, especially if you accept payment in different currencies. It's important to note that Paypal, Eway, and Stripe incur a small transaction fee

LEGAL REQUIREMENTS AND SUPPORT

When setting up a new business, there are several things you need to do for tax and legal purposes. For example, in Australia, where I live, new business owners need to register their business name and apply for an Australian Business Registration Number (ABN). So, please check your country's business and visa requirements for setting up a business and working as a freelancer.

Unsure Whether To Register A Company Name Or Personal Name?

A business name may change over the years, whereas your actual name will not (unless you get married or divorced). If you plan to scale your virtual business, such as bring on team members, you may consider a company name. On the other hand, consider registering your name if you plan to remain the primary service provider for your business. You can change your business name or register a new one in the future if required.

Tax Declaration

As well as registering your business name, you must ensure your tax details are up to date relating to your National Insurance, Social Security, or Tax Reference Number, depending on your country. As a freelancer, your accounting must be organised throughout the year in preparation for the end of the fiscal (financial) year tax returns.

- o In Australia, the fiscal year is from 1 July to 30 June.
- o In the United States, the financial year is from 1 July to 30 June.
- o In the United Kingdom, the financial year runs from 1 April to 31 March for corporation tax and government financial statements. However, for the self-employed and others who pay personal taxation, the fiscal year starts on 6 April.

I highly recommend hiring an accountant to do your tax return forms as they can be more complicated when self-employed versus when paid by an employer.

Legal Documents

As a business owner, you will require a Client Contract (as mentioned above) and Terms and Conditions. T&Cs are basic terms for your business and clarify the professional working relationship between you and the client. These terms should include:

- o the nature of the working relationship, e.g. the client is hiring you as a service provider
- o the hours you work during the week
- o your payment terms and refund policy
- o a standard confidentiality clause

Some other legal documents you may require as your business evolves:

- o Privacy Policy - This is a statement that discloses the ways you gather, use and disclose the client's data.
- o Disclaimer - This is a defensive measure, generally used with the purpose of protection from unwanted claims or liability.
- o Referral Agreement – an agreement for a referral relationship with another freelancer or business that includes a monetary exchange.
- o Trademark - to register your business name or logo legally.

When I began The Healthy VA business, I created my Terms & Conditions as a starting point to set the intention between myself and my clients from the very beginning. I added these terms and conditions to my website and directed clients to the page from their contract. As the business evolved, I hired a Lawyer to create an official T&Cs document, a Privacy Policy, Disclaimer, and eventually Trademarked the business name.

Finding legal support isn't as expensive as it may seem. These days, there are affordable options for small business owners, including Legal Zoom in the US and Progressive Legal in Australia. Please check your country's legal requirements for business owners and search for lawyers who service entrepreneurs and small business.

INSURANCE OPTIONS FOR VIRTUAL ASSISTANTS

There are several types of insurance you can purchase for your business. The most applicable to freelancers would be Professional Liability insurance which covers claims of negligence, claims or slander arising from your work for the client, claims that arise from subcontracting and punitive damages, etc.

General Liability insurance covers third parties such as injury claims, property damage, loss of data due to equipment damage, etc. It is, therefore, only necessary if you work with clients in person. However, most freelancers work remotely and therefore have a low risk of needing this type of insurance.

Business Owners Insurance is also available and combines general liability with protection for your business equipment and data. However, office equipment, such as your laptop, etc., are likely to be included under your property insurance, so again, this insurance may not be a necessity.

ESSENTIAL TOOLS FOR MANAGING YOUR ONLINE BUSINESS

There will be many online tools you'll need to manage and promote your virtual business. However, in the beginning, I recommend keeping your business lean and avoiding any unnecessary expenses. Take advantage of free trials and free subscription options for just the essential tools required. Here are some of the essential tools I recommend:

Communication Tools

GSuite

GSuite includes Gmail, a professional email inbox with your business name (e.g. yourname@businessname.com), an online calendar, and a host of other Google business features.

Google Hangouts

Google Hangouts is included as part of GSuite and is an excellent way to speak with clients via video conference.

Zoom

Zoom is another favourite video conferencing tool as I find the connection is more efficient than using Skype or Google Hangouts. It's a good option if you're holding a meeting with two or more people and need to record the session.

Payment Tools

Paypal

As mentioned in previous chapters, Paypal is a gateway to help you get paid. You may already have a personal Paypal account for shopping online. However, to be paid by others, you need to upgrade to a Business Account, which is free and involves completing a form and providing copies of your ID for money laundering regulations. Once you've upgraded, you can send invoices and request payments. All payments incur a transaction fee and bank processing fee.

Organisation Tools

Asana

Asana is a great task management system that is free to use. It offers a browser and phone app and allows you to organise tasks, To-Do lists, and projects, all with colour coding and due dates. It's an organiser's dream!

Google Drive

A cloud-based storage system (aka an online filing cabinet) and part of the GSuite package. I highly recommend this being your primary place for storing all your files and folders so you can access them from anywhere in the world using just a computer and wifi (the best way to be location independent). Plus, it's more secure than saving documents to your hard drive, where you risk your computer crashing or being stolen.

Lastpass

Lastpass is a password manager and an excellent tool for storing client passwords securely.

5 MUST-KNOW TOOLS TO OFFER A GREAT SERVICE

Each client you work with will have their preferred tools and online systems to manage their business. Here are some of the most common tools you should be aware of. Take advantage of the free trials to learn how to navigate some of the standard features.

Office 360 & GSuite

I mentioned GSuite above as a recommended office tool for your business. Another standard tool is Office 365 by Microsoft. If you've worked in corporate before, you may already have experience with Office 365 features, including Outlook, Word, Excel, and Powerpoint. Most business owners will use one suite or the other, so it's a good idea to grasp the functions in both suites, so you can confidently share files and collaborate.

Mailchimp Newsletters

www.mailchimp.com

Mailchimp is an affordable, user-friendly email newsletter program and a popular tool amongst the small business community. I recommend learning how to set up newsletter templates, campaigns, and autoresponders as this is a common request for Virtual Assistants. Go to www.thehealthyva.com/book-resources to access my Mailchimp video tutorial.

Canva

www.canva.com

Canva provides a fantastic, user-friendly graphic design tool for creating posters, PDF documents, business cards, presentations, and social media images. A must-have for every VA who lacks skills in Adobe Photoshop.

WordPress

www.wordpress.com

I highly recommend gaining foundational knowledge on using WordPress as it's one of the most popular website platforms amongst small business owners. You don't need to learn how to set up a website from scratch or know how to fix technical errors (unless you're tech-savvy and want to an advanced service). Instead, I recommend Virtual Assistants learn their way around a WordPress dashboard, so you can support clients with basic tasks, including how to:

- o set up and publish a blog post
- o create a new webpage

- o edit website copy
- o add new images
- o update plugins and themes.

MARKETING YOUR VIRTUAL ASSISTANT BUSINESS

STARTING WITH YOUR INNER NETWORK

When you're ready to start working with clients, your inner network is the first people to reach out to. These are your friends, family, ex-work colleagues, acquaintances, neighbours, etc., especially those you know who are working in or have connections in the health industry. Start by sharing a post on social media and sending a personal email saying:

'I am now working as a Virtual Assistant – providing admin, creative and technical support for health & wellness businesses. If you know anyone in the industry needing virtual assistant support, please pass on my email address and website for further info. I'd love to help.'

The best way to attract clients is to start from your inner network and expand from there. Recommendations and referrals are so powerful. You may not receive a flood of clients instantly but putting yourself out there will open opportunities going forward. If you find yourself hesitating to tell people what you do or waiting for the perfect moment to share your news, know that hesitation often comes from a place of fear and uncertainty. The point to focus on is - if you don't tell people what you do, how will they know you can help them?

IDENTIFYING YOUR TARGET AUDIENCE

To find and attract clients, you need to know who you want to work with. Every decision you make in your business relies on the knowledge of who you want to support. The health & wellness industry is a niche, yet it is still broad. For example, within the industry, there are numerous categories of business, including:

- o Holistic health - Nutritionists, Naturopaths, Health Coaches.
- o Alternative health - acupuncturists, healers, massage therapists, meditation teachers.
- o Fitness - personal trainers, gyms, yoga, and Pilates instructors/ studios.
- o Medical and occupational health - General Practitioners.

o Physiotherapists, Chiropractors, and other specialist therapies.

o Not-for-profit - charities and health initiatives/

o Retail - online/local health food stores, food production, and organic skincare, etc.

Each business will range in size, location, and experience and therefore operate uniquely and seek different levels of virtual support. You can choose to target any business within the health & wellness space or narrow down your niche further to 'Virtual Assistant for Medical Practices' or 'Virtual Assistant for Naturopaths'.

How Do You Relate To Your Target Audience?

At the start of my Virtual Assistant career, I worked with many health businesses and entrepreneurs from the list above, all at different places in their business journey. After a while, I began to narrow down my target audience even further, based on who I enjoyed working with the most and whose businesses I felt more aligned to. I went from saying 'YES' to every enquiry to serving only two types of clients:

o Target Audience 1 - Well-established entrepreneurs in the health space who were leaders in the industry.

o Target Audience 2 – Newly graduated health coaches from the Institute for Integrative Nutrition who struggled to set up the online side of their business.

For audience 1, I was able to keep up with their pace, enjoyed providing more advanced tech support, and seemed to resonate with how they were leading the way in their field, much like how I was in the virtual assistant space. With audience 2, I resonated with them as I was once in their shoes, finding my way as a new Health Coach many years before. By identifying my two key audiences, I aligned my marketing to speak directly to them, so it became clear who I served, making it easier to attract them to my business.

Adapt Your Marketing

Clarifying your target audience is a working progress. So, my recommendation is to start working with the health & wellness industry as a whole. If, after time, you wish to target a particular type of business within the industry, then do so by looking at:

- o What kind of businesses appeal to you?
- o What experience have you had that relates to them?
- o Who are you in contact with the most?
- o Who are you organically attracting to your business?
- o Are there any trends/similarities between them?
- o Have you noticed people you work better with versus others?

Once you start to summarise who your preferred target audience is, you can actively seek out those businesses and promote your VA services in a manner that appeals to their needs.

Tailor Your Services To Meet Their Needs

Not all health business owners will require the same level of support. So, as well as aligning your marketing to your target audience, tailor your services to their needs too. For example, for audience 1, I tailored a service that focused on monthly VA support because not only did they have the consistent income to pay for it, but an increasing workload for ongoing assistance. For audience 2 (newly graduated Health Coaches), I offered single jobs and short-term projects so I could meet their smaller budgets. As a result, these Health Coaches kept coming back for more, and when they started seeing consistent income, they levelled up to my monthly support option.

WHY EVERY VIRTUAL ASSISTANT SHOULD BE ON LINKEDIN

Linkedin is a business-focused social networking site. An online hub of business activity with hundreds of companies and entrepreneurs using this site to make professional connections and search/ recruit for jobs. Think of Linkedin like Facebook but in a more professional manner.

You may already have a profile for your previous or current employment. If you are currently employed and setting up your VA business as a side hustle, it may not be appropriate to update your Linkedin profile at this stage. So, please use your discretion. If you are ready to display your new business and career publicly, Linkedin is a great platform to join.

6 Steps to Creating a Great Linkedin Profile

1. Add A Professional Photo

You don't need a professional headshot, just a bright and clear photo of you smiling, from the shoulders up. Ask a friend to take it for you or take a selfie looking straight towards the camera. No pouting!

2. Make Your Headline Stand Out

Your headline is the sentence that sits under your name in your profile and what viewers see in the newsfeed when you post, share, and comment. Therefore, you want it to be short and specific. Here are a couple of examples that speak directly to your audience:

- o Virtual Assistant for the Health & Wellness industry.
- o Virtual Assistant supporting Health & Wellness businesses.
- o Virtual Sidekick for Health Business Owners.

3. Keep Your Work History Relevant

You don't need to list every job you ever had on your profile. Instead, only list the relevant jobs to the admin, creative and technical support you'll provide as a VA.

4. Add Your Education

Add your school/college experience and any additional certifications that would be relevant for your VA business

5. Add A Summary, But Keep It Focused On Your Clients

The summary section is less about you and your experience and more about how you can help your clients. It should be brief (max 200 words) and answer the following questions:

- What do you do?
- How can you help?
- What is the best way to contact you?

For example:

'I'm a Virtual Assistant offering reliable and affordable support services to health business owners.

I take care of the day-to-day online tasks to focus on the work they love and do best.

The best way to contact me is by email:

name@businessname.com'

6. Add Your Website URL

When your website is ready, add your URL to your profile so readers can find out more about you and your services.

Once you have your profile ready, start searching and connecting with other business owners and associates in the health and wellness industry. Also, connect with other Virtual Assistants, old work colleagues (if appropriate), friends, and acquaintances. Once connected, share a short 'hello, thanks for connecting' message as a polite introduction. Here, you will start building connections and expose yourself to an extended network of potential clients.

Ask For Recommendations

The Recommendations section of your profile acts like testimonials. Reach out to past colleagues an

d managers you've connected with (if appropriate) via the Recommendations section on your profile and ask that they write one for you. Do the same for your VA clients after you've finished working with them, so your profile is filled with positive affirmations and support for your work. You can also copy and paste the client recommendations onto your website testimonial page (see next chapter).

Dip in and out of Linkedin weekly and engage with other people's comments and posts in the newsfeed - similar to how you would approach Facebook, however, keep your posts relevant to the platform with a business focus. Also, don't be afraid to reach out to health business owners and ask them directly if they need any VA support. You never know; you may be exactly who they are looking for!

CREATING A SIMPLE FIRST WEBSITE

Your website is your online home, a place readers can go to find out more about you and your VA services. It will be a website you will update numerous times throughout your career and as your VA business evolves. Therefore, you should keep it simple from the beginning.

Creating a basic yet beautiful website is very affordable these days and something you can do yourself without hiring a web developer. I recommend building your own website, so you gain experience of the process, in case you wish to offer website services in the future. My favourite website platform is Squarespace (www.squarespace.com), a platform that offers pre-made templates where you can add your text and images. It is easy to navigate, even for website beginners, and they have a comprehensive library of customer support information. You can also purchase your website domain (e.g. www.businessname.com) through

Squarespace, and the platform subscription price includes website hosting and security backup.

Your Website Structure

For a Virtual Assistant website, you need the following pages:

- ○ Home page – include a headline, a summary about who you are, an image of you, and links to your services page and about page.
- ○ About Page – a summary about who you are, your experience, and, more importantly, how you can help.
- ○ Services Page – here you list the VA services you offer, for example, a brief description of Single jobs and Monthly work. You may also like to add your rates on this page; however, this is not necessary.
- ○ Contact Page – either a contact form or your best contact details.
- ○ Testimonial page - a list of testimonials from previous clients.

Optional pages:

- ○ Blog Posts – If you'd like a blog on your VA website, ensure the content is relevant for your target audience and your business – e.g. 'productivity tips for health business owners'.

It's essential to let go of any perfectionist tendencies here. Know that the perfect website does not exist. Your main goal is to create an online home that readers can visit to learn more about you and your services.

6 PLACES TO FIND VIRTUAL ASSISTANT JOBS

A great way to find clients is to spread your profile over several key platforms to gain more exposure and access to jobs. Promote yourself independently through social media and your website, but also use these additional platforms to position yourself in front of potential clients and apply for jobs.

Upwork

www.upwork.com

Freelancer

www.freelancer.com

Two popular, global freelancing sites for finding short term and long-term projects. You can search and bid for jobs based on your specific skills and be invited by clients to apply for jobs. All time tracking, contracts, and payments are handled via the platforms, therefore, you pay a small percentage of your hourly rate for each project. The more success you have with projects, the greater your feedback rating and exposure to new clients. These are great options for hassle-free job search and client liaison. However, as they are global platforms, there is a lot of competition. Often clients expect to pay less on these sites than they would if they hired a VA directly.

Facebook Groups For Business

I recommend joining Facebook groups for 'health entrepreneurs', 'solo entrepreneurs' or 'women in business' etc. Use them to connect with like-minded people, and if there's an enquiry about Virtual Assistance or a question about various tasks and tools you have experience with, then offer your guidance and share what you do. There are strict guidelines for Facebook groups, as many people have used them to pitch and sell their services when not appropriate. However, if you approach these online communities the right way, there can be opportunities to make good connections and future referrals.

Facebook Groups For Virtual Assistants

There are also many groups on Facebook and Linkedin specifically for Virtual Assistants where members often share job notices.

The Freelance Collective

www.thefreelancecollective.com.au (Australia Only)

A fantastic online community of Australian freelancers, available for a monthly membership and includes a private Facebook Group and public Directory. Many clients visit their site to search for freelancers, and job notices are posted in their private Facebook group. If you don't live in Australia, search for similar freelance communities in your local area.

Fiverr

www.fiverr.com

Fiverr is a similar site to Upwork and Freelancer, but instead of clients displaying job notices, the freelancers show what they offer with a three-level pricing option. The services you offer can be hourly VA services (5 hours, 10 hours, or 20 hours) or specific jobs such as:

- o Data Entry – 3 hours, 5 hours, or 10 hours.
- o Social Media scheduling – 7 posts, 14 posts, 30 posts.
- o Copyediting blog posts – 500 words, 1000 words, 2000 words.

Pricing is competitive, so you may need to offer lower than your standard rates.

CREATING POSITIVE CLIENT RELATIONSHIPS

FIRST IMPRESSIONS MATTER

When receiving a client inquiry, they may come through your website, Linkedin page, referral, or other social media page. Regardless, before you agree to work with a client, I recommend arranging an initial video call. See it as a short interview, no more than 20 minutes long, and an opportunity to discuss their business, your VA services, your rates and how you can best support them. You're interviewing the client just as much as they are interviewing you. They should be a good fit for your business and a pleasure to work with.

Here are some key questions to explore during your initial chat. You don't have to ask them all; just choose several questions to help get to know them better. These open-ended questions can provide a better insight into a client's business, how they work and who they are:

o   What's your reason for needing support with your business?

o   How are you currently managing the business?

o   Have you worked with Virtual Assistant before?

o   What are you finding the most challenging?

o   What problems do you have at the moment?

o   If you could overcome these challenges, how would your business differ?

o   If we worked together, how do you think I would help your business?

o   What do you want your business to look like in 1 year?

o   For how long do you see us working together?

o   What's your preferred way to communicate? Email/Phone etc.

o   What are your top 3 goals for the next 6 months?

o   If we began working together, what would be your top priorities?

o   Do you already have processes and procedures for your business?

o   Why did you become a [insert occupation]/start your business?

o   Who are your target audience?

o   What services do you provide?

o   How many clients do you have at the moment?

o   Where did you hear about me?

By the end of the call, you should both have come to a decision whether you would like to work together or not.

Discussing Your Rates And Services

When you enter your initial client conversation ('interview'), ensure you have a clear understanding of the services you provide and how much you charge so you feel and sound confident when offering your support. If a client objects to your rates, avoid bartering with your time and value. You don't have to reduce your rates to meet someone else's needs. There will be other clients who can afford your services and value your time.

Many Virtual Assistants choose to display their rates on their website, so potential clients are aware of costs upfront. However, a service's value is often miscommunicated when rates are displayed publicly, without an initial conversation about the client's specific needs. It's a personal choice, and if you decide to display your rates online, I recommend displaying a 'From' price, as this will at least allow more flexibility when quoting work – e.g. 'Virtual Assistant services from $40 per hour.'

Complete The Booking Process

When you and a client have agreed to work together, send out a contract and the first invoice within 24-48 hours to lock in the agreement (while also demonstrating your efficiency and organisation skills!). Visit www.thehealthyva.com/book-resources for an Invoice template.

Once a client has signed a contract and processed the first payment or deposit, I recommend sending a 'welcome email' to say how excited you are to start working with them and reconfirm the start date – a nice gesture to start the relationship on an upbeat track. Follow this same onboarding procedure for each new client so it becomes a standard business process. And lastly, congratulations!

THE HEALTHY VA

Celebrate each new client with a cheer, pat on the back, and perhaps a glass of champagne!

CREATING LONG-LASTING RELATIONSHIPS

Developing long-term relationships with clients is a fantastic way to generate recurring revenue and grow your business. You can become an essential part of their team if you invest in the relationship from the beginning. The best way to maintain positive relationships is to keep communication open and ask for feedback often. I recommend sending feedback questions to clients at the 3-month mark to ensure they are satisfied with their support and if there's any way you can improve your services. Questions can include:

- o How satisfied are you with my Virtual Assistant support (on a scale of 1-5)?
- o What are you enjoying most about having a Virtual Assistant?
- o Are there any areas of improvement in my services?

o Are there any additional areas in your business you need support with?

o Do you have any ideas on how we can improve our working relationship?

If you work with a client for over 12 months, celebrate your 1-year anniversary. Send your client a small gesture of your appreciation. By choosing you as their virtual support, they are supporting your business too. Here are some healthy gift ideas:

o Fruit/Veg hamper
o Bunch of native flowers
o Gift voucher for an online health store
o Chocolates (because who doesn't like chocolate!)

TERMINATING CLIENT CONTRACTS

Most clients will be fabulous to work with. However, there may be a time where communication breaks down or a particular client is challenging. I've had clients try to micro-manage, question every invoice they receive and take ages to respond to my emails, while complaining that work is delayed. I've also had clients expect me to respond at all hours of the day and night, and demand urgent turnaround for insignificant tasks. Overtime, I've learnt how to manage these interactions confidently and how to professionally terminate a contract so the client can find someone else to work with who is more suited to their needs and working style.

Creating boundaries at the beginning of your working relationship will help to avoid miscommunication and client issues. Clarifying things like your working hours, business processes, and turnaround times in your T&Cs and during initial conversations will set expectations for your relationship from the start. From my experience, if a potential client is challenging during your first encounter (for example, during your introduction call or initial email correspondence), there's a high chance they'll be challenging to work with ongoing.

If you need to terminate a client contract early, visit www.thehealthyva.com/book-resources to download two email templates you can use to let them go gently. Maintaining integrity and professionalism in your business is essential for a positive reputation.

YOUR VA CAREER & BEYOND

COLLABORATING WITH OTHER FREELANCERS

Collaborating with other freelancers can be an excellent opportunity to increase your client base. Ideally, you will collaborate with people who offer services and skills that complement your own. For example, as a Virtual Assistant, I often collaborated with a Brand Strategist who I met at a networking event. After connecting online, we noticed we had a similar work ethic and style. So, when a project came about from a client who needed both our skills, one of us recommended the other, and we worked together for the first time. From there, our working relationship began.

If you'd like to find other freelancers to collaborate with, network offline and online in spaces that connect you to other freelancers. Also, when working with clients who are using other freelancers (like a web developer or graphic designer), connect with them once the project is complete to see if you'd both like to work together again in the future.

THE HEALTHY VA

Collaboration options

You can collaborate on a referral basis where you refer each other to your clients should they need the complimentary services. Then liaise with the client separately about your rates and contract terms. This way, you are working 'alongside' each other to meet the client's requirements. The client pays you both separately, and there is no legal contract or conditions required between the two of you. An alternative collaboration would be to offer a service together, which would be regarded as a strategic partnership, with each person having an equal share of responsibility, contribution, and reward. This relationship would require a legal contract and terms & conditions.

I recommend referral collaborations over strategic partnerships as you're not contractually bound to someone else, their business, or their reputation. However, it doesn't mean a strategic partnership isn't a good option. If you can foresee a long working relationship and can create in-demand services together, then a contractual arrangement may be your best option.

FUTURE CAREER OPPORTUNITIES FOR VIRTUAL ASSISTANTS

After several years of working as a Virtual Assistant, I transitioned into a Marketing and Operations Consultant, offering strategy and implementation. My experience and knowledge had evolved to be able to offer this service on a day rate basis, significantly increasing my income. As you develop your skills as a Virtual Assistant, you may also feel drawn to working with a favourite system, business area or project. Over time, with more experience and additional training, you can progress your career to offer a specific service and charge higher rates for 'specialist' skills. Here are six specialist services to consider:

Online Course Assistant

Do you love supporting clients with their online programs? Can you build membership sites on platforms like

Teachable and Udemy? Perhaps you'd like to become a specialist in creating online programs and courses, offering a service that manages the project from start to finish. This could include developing the sales page, planning the launch, setting up the membership site, managing the program, and providing customer service to members while the client focuses on delivering their content.

Marketing Assistant

Do you enjoy helping clients to set up their marketing funnels to attract new customers? Why not expand your knowledge in this area by learning proven marketing techniques to offer specialist marketing services.

Website Builder

Are you a whiz on websites and feel comfortable setting up online stores and membership sites? As a new business owner, having a website created can be confusing, not knowing where to start and how it works. Perhaps you could provide a trustworthy, affordable solution, offering guidance on creating a stylish yet simple website for their business?

Social Media Strategist

Support with social media is one of the most popular requests from health business owners, especially when it comes to daily management, setting up social media tools, and creating Facebook and Instagram adverts. If you love social media, perhaps you'd like to study the various platforms in detail, learn how to create effective ads, and offer this service as a 'Social Media Strategist'.

Webinar Specialist

Webinars are increasingly popular for business owners, whether they use them for marketing purposes or to educate current clients. Becoming the Go-To person for webinar support is an excellent option for a Virtual Assistant. It will require an understanding of how to set up a webinar tool and all its features, being a secondary host, and preparing for common technical glitches during live events.

CRM Specialist

Customer Relationship Management (CRM) tools offer the complete package for managing an online business. Infusionsoft and Ontraport are two popular systems that offer opportunities to become 'consultants' and software affiliates. By learning these tools inside and out, you could consider becoming an 'Ontraport VA', for example, and charge higher rates per hour to manage someone's account and gain referral rewards as an affiliate of the software.

TIME TO GET STARTED

This book has provided the knowledge you need to create a thriving Virtual Assistant business. Now, it's time to start! The next step can be the most challenging, not knowing what to focus on first. So, I've created Your First Month Checklist to provide some direction and accountability. Visit www.thehealthyva.com/book-resources to download the checklist. Whether you want to become a Virtual Assistant full time or as a side hustle to your primary job, this book and checklist provide clear insight and direction for setting up your VA business and start seeing clients within one month.

Wishing you the best of luck.

ABOUT THE AUTHOR

Joanna Mitchell is a writer based in Sydney, Australia. In 2013, she created The Healthy VA, offering Virtual Assistant services for the health and wellness industry, the first of its kind. As a result, she became recognised as the 'Go-To' VA for health businesses in Australia. Since evolving The Healthy VA into an educational blog for aspiring freelancers, Joanna has worked as Marketing Consultant and Copywriter. Today, she writes about parenting, business, and self-development on Medium and other online publications. When she's not tapping away at her keyboard, you'll find her chasing after her active little boy at the beach.

ONE LAST THING...

Thank you so much for reading this book.

I would really appreciate it if you would please review this book on Amazon. Whether you thought it was great, terrible, or anywhere in between, I'd love to have your feedback.

Reviews are the best way for an author like me to get discovered. Readers like you can help make it happen.

Thanks in advance,
Joanna Mitchell

Printed in Great Britain
by Amazon